"Why?"

Our Magnificent Earth!...
Our Ultimate Destiny!

Carl D. Rowe

WESTBOW
PRESS®
A DIVISION OF THOMAS NELSON
& ZONDERVAN

WestBow Press books may be ordered through
booksellers or by contacting:

WestBow Press
A Division of Thomas Nelson & Zondervan
1663 Liberty Drive
Bloomington, IN 47403
www.westbowpress.com
1 (866) 928-1240

Scripture taken from the New King James Version®. Copyright ©
1982 by Thomas Nelson. Used by permission. All rights reserved.

ISBN: 978-1-9736-7694-2 (sc)
ISBN: 978-1-9736-7695-9 (e)

Library of Congress Control Number: 2019915759

Print information available on the last page.

WestBow Press rev. date: 10/11/2019

Preface:

Hey Guys & Gals, got a minute?

Are you into Elk hunting? Fishing? Hiking and Camping? Bird-Watching? If you are you, no doubt, have a real serious appreciation of Nature and the wonder and complexity of it all.

You may be wondering how did all of this come about. Did this magnificent world of ours just happen by an amazing number of miraculous chances?

When you're out there in the mountains, or on the beach and you look up and view the billions of stars and planets and the Milky Way, do you wonder if there's really a God who created all of this, and maybe me as well?

You would really like to know a lot more about Creation and God, but you are turned off by organized religion? Good News! God is not interested in religion, but desires to have a personal relationship with you, one of His Children.

Please stay with me and read through this short book. I want to describe to you how this Earth came into being and how God has provided every conceivable resource that was needed by man, and then provided a way that we might dwell with Him forever.

I wish that I could present an impressive list of my credentials, university degrees, books authored, and literary accomplishments. Truth is that I possess none of the above. I happen to be a simple man who loves God and God's creation and desires to awaken the wonder of His creation in everyone who may read this.

Wherever you may be on your spiritual journey, I hope that you will be challenged to open up your heart and mind to the real possibility of a Creator / God who loves you and desires a relationship with you. This is not an in-depth discussion of theology. I am, in no way, qualified to tackle that subject. I do, however, have the God-given gifts of sight, hearing, touching, feeling, observing, and a sense of awe at the awesomeness of, the beauty and complexity of nature, all of which point to our Creator.

The scientific community would have us believe that there is a logical, scientific explanation for everything. My eyes, my senses, my mind, and spirit tell me otherwise. So, I raise a number of questions, "WHY?" and present my take on **why things are as they are.**

Enjoy!
Carl D. Rowe

Dedication:

This book is dedicated to my Wonderful Wife of 62 years, Virginia Rowe, and to our children, Winston, Warren, Mar'ti, Holly, and David Wilder, who is in Heaven. Our Grandchildren, David, Bradley, Annabelle, Brittany, Jade, Valerie, Olivia, Ian, Grace, Wilder, Ginessa, Summer, Allie, Nicolette, Carleigh, Genevieve, and Levi. Also, to our wonderful Daughter-In-Law, Missy Rowe and to our awesome Sons-In-Law, Joseph Baldwin, and Dave Thomas and to Granddaughter Brittany's Husband, Ian Martin and their children, Stephani and Silas. Last, but certainly not least, our Grandsons' wives, David's Casey, their four children, Leah Grace, Elliana, Jon David & Lilah, Bradley's wife Bria, their son Winston B., Carleigh's Nick and their baby boy, Vinnie, and Nicolette's Harrell.

Contents

Chapter 1

The Earth, Our Home in Space

The six things that stand out, in my mind, as I contemplate the greatness of God are order creativity, diversity, symmetry, harmony, and intelligence.

Regarding Order, the most obvious manifestation, of course, is the visible universe, including the sun, moon, stars, Earth and the planets in their orbits.

In simplistic terms, the Earth was placed in an orbit around the sun, at the perfect distance from the sun, so that human life could exist and flourish and not be burned up or frozen by these extreme temperatures. Simultaneously, God created the moon and placed it in the perfect orbit around the Earth. Because of the rotations of the Earth, sun, and moon, and the slight tilt of the Earth on its axis, we have day and night and an accurate

1

system of time. This is what provides a rhythm of life (e.g., sleeping, working, and playing). Gravity holds our solar system's objects in place, in their precise orbits at all times, but who created Gravity?

Colossians 1:16-17 tells us, in no uncertain terms!

> "For by Him all things were created; things in Heaven and Earth, visible and invisible, whether thrones or powers or rulers or authorities; all things were created by Him and for Him. He is before all things and in Him all things HOLD TOGETHER"

The universe, of course, is unfathomable in its enormity, splendor, and complexity. The Earth is our "home in space" in this vast universe, created by Almighty God for His pleasure and for His creatures. The Creator, in His wisdom and power, provided every conceivable resource needed by Man within and upon the surface of the Earth.

Can you visualize that the above scenario just happened accidentally? Or was there an Intelligence, a Creator, an all-powerful God who made all of this happen? I am totally aware of all the scientific "evidence" out there that seeks to discredit God and to exalt man. I do believe in science and technology up to a point and do not see any real conflict between religion and science, but it is God who imparts all knowledge and understanding to men. There is nothing new in this universe, or on this planet. All inventions and discoveries eventually utilize resources and materials and elements that have always been here since the dawn of creation.

"Just the Facts, Maam"

The scientific community claims to deal with "facts" and clamors for "visual evidence" to support the claims of Christianity versus science. I submit the following: We are here! Our Earth is real! Our environment "is what it is." Scientific theories can be and should be, questioned, but the natural world cannot be questioned. All we have to do is look around and explore the marvelous creation and wonders of nature that defy all logic and scientific knowledge. In subsequent chapters, amazing details of the Earth, including plant and animal kingdoms, will be presented.

Is there really a God, a Creator of the Earth and our vast universe? Or are science and technology our gods and do they have all the answers? On subjects on which they have no answers, they create theories and declare them as "facts."

Every new "discovery" and every new "theory" that science comes up with inevitably raises even more unanswered questions, so the quest never ends. Some scientists admit, "the more we know, the more we discover how much we don't know." With questions such as, How did the universe begin? and How did human life begin? The honest scientist admits, "We don't really know!

Even as I write this, there is a new theory out there called "biocentrism," which seeks to negate and replace all previous theories with a lot of nonsensical babblings regarding "consciousness." By the way, God is nowhere to be found, but the author of this theory is being lauded as "brilliant."

There are, of course, numerous theories that range from the ridiculous to the plausible, regarding how the Earth and the universe began. These exclude any mention of God and go to great lengths to prove their points. It's as if they would rather stand on their heads, jump through hoops, and do cartwheels than use the forbidden word, God.

I will share where I, personally stand regarding creation and the origin of humankind. The following excerpt from an article entitled "Changing Views of Science and Scripture" by Bernard Ramm (March 1992) is closely in line with my thinking.

> "Almighty God is Creator, World Ground, and Omnipotent Sustainer. In His mind, the entire plan of creation was formed with Man as the climax. Over the millions of years of geological history, the Earth is

prepared for man's dwelling, or as it has been put by others, the cosmos was pregnant with man. From time to time, the great creative acts, *de novo*, took place. The complexity of animal forms increased. Finally, he whom all creation anticipated is made, MAN, in whom alone is the breath of God."

"Attention, Class."

If you are a student of science, you have been taught that the following "laws" and "theories" explain in great detail, the origin of the universe, humankind, animals, and the rest of the natural world. According to science, "laws" are considered "absolutes" that are irrefutable because of repeated experimentation over a long period of time, producing the same result. "Theories," however, are deemed "almost laws" but haven't really stood the test of time and continued experimentation. Then there are the "hypotheses" and the "postulates," which I would classify as "wild guesses."

➢ The big bang theory (widely accepted by secular science, but losing traction) claims that in this vast sea of nothingness, there was a "point" or "singularity" that exploded, thereby creating the universe, which has continually expanded. What was this so-called "point"? Where did it come from? It didn't come from the Earth, or the sea since the Earth or the sea did not exist at this point. So, what ignited it? Since there was only "nothingness," there could be no "point" to ignite and no source of fire to ignite it. Are we supposed to believe this?

Another "explanation" of the "big bang theory" is that there wasn't an explosion in space, but it was **space itself** that exploded, thereby creating the universe, which is continually expanding. Space is, of course, infinite and is comprised of "nothingness." To state that space, over time, kept compressing itself until it finally compressed into a single point that exploded, makes no sense. Nothing is still nothing, and space is still infinite and can't be compressed. Also, I might add that the age of the universe has been changed dozens of times. Read "Changing Views of the History of the Earth" by Richard Harter (1998 – 2005). Science estimates the age of the universe at 14 billion years.

Translation: "Yeah, right!! Everything from Nothing!"

Other hypotheses and postulates include the following:

- ➢ Hubbell's law of expansion
- ➢ Kepler's law of planetary motion
- ➢ Newton's law of motion
- ➢ The universal law of gravitation
- ➢ Laws of thermodynamics
- ➢ Archimedes principle of buoyancy
- ➢ Evolution and natural selection
- ➢ The theory of general relativity
- ➢ Heisenberg's Uncertainty Principle

I have a new law to introduce here! It's titled **"Carl's Law."** It simply states, <u>**"You can't get something from nothing**</u>." Why not? It's my book, my call. No science needed, just good old logic.

We know that everything that exists on Earth is made up of matter, which is either in the form of a liquid, a solid, or a gas. Matter cannot be created or destroyed. It can only be changed from one form to another. I repeat my earlier comment that there is nothing new on this Earth. All Inventions and discoveries eventually utilize resources, materials, and elements that have always been here from the dawn of creation.

"What on Earth!"

So, God, having created the Earth (in whatever period of time it took) infused His creation with an infinite variety of resources and in vastly amazing quantities, so that humans, His crowning glory, would have everything they needed for not only survival but enjoyment as well. What, exactly, were these resources? Let's begin with the atmosphere.

The Atmosphere:

The human body must have oxygen in order to survive and flourish. No problem! The layer of atmosphere in which we live is largely oxygen and hydrogen. Thank You, Lord! The higher one goes, the thinner the air, making it harder and harder to breathe. Beyond the atmosphere, there is no oxygen. Science calls this level the stratosphere, and beyond that is what is called space, where there is no gravity. Thankfully, this gigantic "bubble" surrounding the Earth is our shield from harmful rays that would otherwise make life impossible. Guess who thought of this and made it happen? Equally important, the atmosphere and its layer of ozone, is what controls all weather on the Earth. The atmosphere produces rain (our automatic sprinkler system) and snow that fills our oceans, rivers, and lakes.

The Sky:

The sky provides us with a covering of beauty, and, more importantly, protection from harmful rays. The clouds provide beauty and shade from the sun. At night, we are privileged to view the glory and complexity of the universe with its infinite array of stars, planets, comets, magnificent sunrises and sunsets, the northern lights and, of course, the moon. The moon has three purposes as I see it. A "lesser light" for the Earth, controls the ocean tides and contributes to romances. How many love songs mention "moonlight?" We are even privileged to witness the power of lightning in times of storm.

> "When I gaze into the Night Sky and see the work of your fingers. The Stars and Moon suspended in space, what is Man, oh what is Man, that You are mindful of Him?" Psalms 8: 3-5

As far as we know, the Earth is the only planet in the universe that possesses the resource of water. (Science is now reporting that that water has been found on the planet Mars, in the form of ice.) Since the average surface temperature on Mars varies from minus 80 degrees Fahrenheit to minus 195 degrees, it will remain frozen until heat from some source is applied, which will require expending energy to melt it, and where will that energy come from? Water, of course, is critical for sustaining all life on the Earth. Our Earth is approximately 70 percent covered with ocean water. On the surface of the Earth, there are countless rivers and lakes, and underneath the surface, there are vast aquifers of pure drinking water. It is this combination of air, sunlight, and water, and a process called photosynthesis that causes all plant life to grow and flourish. Are these amazing facts just coincidental?

Obviously, without plant life, there would be no vegetables, fruits, flowers, or even meats, since the animals could not exist without food and water.

The Sea:

Our Earth has 4 major oceans covering its surface, namely, the Atlantic, The Pacific, the Indian, and the Artic oceans, that are referred to as the World Ocean. The World Ocean covers 99%of the biosphere and it is estimated that we have only seen and explored 5% of it. The ocean maintains life on earth, regulates earth's temperature, and provides us with oxygen, food, and many other things, such as drinking water, raw materials, and medications.

Additionally, the sea has had a tremendous impact upon all cultures, and is in many works of art, history books, songs and music as well as movies. More and more people are participating in all types of water sports, cruises, etc.

The sea, of course, is teeming with an amazing, unlimited, variety of fish and seafood of all types for our enjoyment. It also offers another means of travel to distant lands, commercial shipping of goods from country to country.

The Surface of the Earth:

As we progress downward from the atmosphere to the sky, to the sea and now to the surface of the Earth, we begin to comprehend the power and majesty of creation and how all the elements of Creation work, in unison, to comprise our amazing Earth.

When we look at the landscape across the surface of the Earth, we are awed by the tremendous variations and diversity of it, ranging from the marshy lowlands to the great plains, to the mountains, to the deserts, and jungles These variations serve to illustrate, vividly, the attributes of our Creator which include diversity, creativity, and intelligence. God has put within every person's DNA the ability to adapt to almost any environment and climate. Humans and animals, therefore, inhabit diverse lands across the globe.

World-famous author, James Michener, in his book "Hawaii," wrote that these islands presented an extremely hostile environment to the first group of arrivals to these shores, but they adapted and overcame their challenges. Other native groups later traveled in large "canoes" to the Hawaiian Islands, bringing with them shoots from plants, vegetables, fruits, and seeds as well as some small animals They began to inhabit the islands and brought along with them their Polynesian culture. You might say that this is an example of "beauty from ashes," since the islands were once just volcanic rock, and they are now incredibly lush and beautiful. This fact is true of many inhabitants of remote environs all over the globe.

What are some of the amazing resources that the creator has provided for us?

Tillable land for growing the food we need for healthy bodies. A list of known vegetables consists of 130 different types. 40 percent of the land in the U.S.A. is used for agriculture. Our major crops are corn, soybeans, wheat, sugar, sugar beets, potatoes, bananas, and coffee.

Consider this: a single ear of corn contains about eight hundred kernels of corn in sixteens rows. If those eight hundred kernels were planted and watered, and tilled, they might produce eight hundred stalks of corn, which may contain sixteen hundred ears of corn, which may result in one million two hundred eighty thousand kernels. If this scenario were carried out to its logical progression, the crop produced would be ridiculously enormous. This is how the Creator multiplies all things to us.

Animals: A major source of protein, necessary for our bodies, of course, comes from animals. The most popular types of meats are beef, pork, chicken, turkey, veal, fish, and kinds of seafood. These meat dishes can be prepared in an unbelievable variety of delectable ways for our health and enjoyment

Another amazing animal is the dairy cow. The cow not only provides us with delicious milk, but the by-products of milk are also amazing! Consider this impressive list of products:

Buttermilk
Butter
Yogurt
Sour Cream
Whipping Cream
Cheese (dozens of types)
Cheese Spreads
Ice Cream

You may have heard this question when you were growing up. "How can a brown cow eat green grass & give white milk, which turns to yellow butter."

I don't know, but it's an interesting question!

Trees: Trees provide lumber used to build our homes. Fruit trees provide a variety of delicious fruits, such as apples, oranges, and peaches. (two thousand types of fruit exist) Trees are the largest plants on the Earth. They give us oxygen, store carbon, stabilize the soil, and give life to the world's wildlife. Additionally, trees provide shade from the sun and possess aesthetic beauty in a variety of brilliant colors.

Carl D. Rowe

Below the Surface of the Earth:

We have touched upon the miraculous things that God has provided for us above, and upon, the face of the Earth, but what about "under the Earth? The basic composition of the Earth consists of the core, the outer core, the mantle, and the crust. For our purposes, we shall only discuss the marvelous aspects of the crust.

There are many things that, over time, reshape the surface of the Earth. Some examples of this are tectonic activity (shifting of tectonic plates), erosion, volcanoes, glaciers, flowing water, and coral reefs. The crust is comprised of three types of rock: igneous, sedimentary, and metamorphic.

Igneous rock is produced by the crystallization and solidification of molten magma. Granite is one example of igneous rock. Sedimentary rock is formed by materials that, over vast periods of time, settle on the floor of the ocean and solidify. Finally, metamorphic rock are those that change, over time, by heat and pressure from an igneous state.

The following facts I find astounding regarding the natural resources the Creator provided for us. Yes, we have to dig and mine to get to them, but they are there for us.

Consider that there exists 92 different types of metals embedded in the Crust of the Earth! How can that be possible? What "explosion" could create even one metal? We won't attempt to enumerate a listing of all of these metals but will consider some of the most important ones to our everyday lives. All metals have specific properties, which determine their value, strength, usefulness, and ability to combine with other metals and chemicals to produce an endless variety of products.

Two basic materials required to construct the structural components of our tall buildings are steel and concrete. We get steel from iron ore, and we make concrete from rock, lime, and water. Our tall buildings could never have been built without these ingredients.

Another very important metal is aluminum. Aluminum is made from a mineral called bauxite and is used in the manufacturing of airplanes, windows, and many other products we use all of the time.

The following are 15 of the most precious metals found within and under the surface of our Earth:

gold / silver / platinum / rutherium / iridium / rhenium / palladum / osmium / bronze / copper / iron / lead / magnesium / tungsten and zinc.

Then there is the glittery stuff. According to Forbes, there are over four thousand minerals on Earth. The rarest and most expensive gemstones are listed below. According to my sources, all of the gemstones listed below are comprised of varying chemical compositions, except diamonds, which are pure carbon.

Jeremejevite $2,000 per carat
Fire Opal 2,300 per carat
Poudretteite 3,000 per carat
Benitoite 4,000 per carat
Musgravite 6,000 per carat
Red Beryl 10,000 per carat
Alexandrite 12,000 per carat
Diamond 15,000 per carat
Serendibite 18,000 per carat
Grandidierite 20,000 per carat
Taaffeite 35,000 per carat
Red Diamond 1,000,000 per carat

"Question of the Day."

How did these minerals of aluminum, borate, oxygen, fluoride, & hydrogen, for example, manage to get together in the exact formula AL6 B5 O15 (F,OH)3 to form the gemstone, Jeremejevite, and only in Siberia?

Underneath the surface of the Earth are vast areas of pure, clean water which are called aquifers. The management of water resources is called hydrology. Groundwater is where we get most of our drinking water, but the make-up and movement of aquifers, along with the management of groundwater, is a complex thing that is extremely important. That is why we have governmental and environmental agencies monitoring and regulating our water resources. Unfortunately, there are countries in desperate need of water, and we need to do whatever we can to help.

Another major resource provided by our Creator also lies beneath the surface of the Earth, and that is oil. Oil is in constant demand all over the world, and wars are being fought to acquire the oil fields. Oil, of course, in the form of gasoline, is required for millions of automobiles, for aviation fuel, for the manufacturing industries, the military establishment, and countless other uses. Without this resource, cars, machines and airplanes would not exist.

"Crude Oil," as it is known in the industry, is pumped up from the ground and transported to oil refineries. There, through an incredibly complex process, it is essentially "boiled." In the boiling process, the crude oil gives off a number of amazing products, at certain temperatures, such as the following:

gasoline / kerosene / diesel fuel / motor oil / liquid petroleum / gas asphalt / naphtha

There exists over two hundred additional products from the derivatives of crude oil. Again, we see the diversity and creativity of the Creator, who does all things well.

Reality Check"

When we look at, and contemplate, our marvelous world, created by God Almighty himself, and the endless resources He provided for us, why would we want to "escape" to a harsh, drab, desolate place millions of miles away from HOME? As our astronauts have dubbed it "The Good Earth."

The two closest planets to us are Mars and Venus. The average distance from Earth to Mars is 33.9 million miles, and the time required to travel there is about 270 Earth days. Why would a crew of astronauts, engineers, and scientists want to spend 270 days (6,480 hours) cooped up in a relatively small spacecraft, eat only pre-packaged "food," with limited water to drink (and for disposal), limited exercise opportunities, sheer boredom and **away from family for 1 and 1/2 years** (remember, the trip home requires the same amount of time and supplies). FOR WHAT? Only to find an extremely hostile environment, basically uninhabitable by human beings without all kinds of equipment and gadgets.

Even if the environment is habitable, which it is not, and water was plentiful, which it is not, and we attempted to build just the beginnings of the structures required to establish a colony there, the logistics of transporting food, workers, and materials to Mars, would take centuries at an astronomical cost.

After all, it cost us $25.4 billion (in 1973 dollars) to put a man on the moon which is only 225,000 miles from Earth. Tragically, it also costs 150 American lives to accomplish that feat. Sure, it felt good, and was a phenomenal accomplishment, but, in reality, what did it accomplish for humankind other than more and better computers, cell phones and bragging rights?

The planet Venus, of course, is the closest one to Earth at only 25 million miles away, with a travel time of 224.7 Earth days. However, the average temperature on the surface of Venus is 870 degrees Fahrenheit. I think we can forget that one, plus it lies under a heavy overcast, permanently.

Ironically, all of this is in vain! There is no Utopia, in space or anywhere else, but we can find peace and contentment in God, through his Son, Jesus Christ. Humankind on any other planet is still humankind, and the evils here on Earth would be the same evils on other planets

In summary, God, in His goodness and mercy, prepared this "home in space" for us, providing every conceivable resource imaginable, only on our Earth out of the trillions of other stars and planets in His universe. And, when the "Fullness of Time" had come, sent His only begotten Son to Earth to show us the way to Himself.

"I will lift up my eyes to the hills, from whence cometh my help. My help cometh from the Lord, who made Heaven and Earth." Psalms: 121

Chapter 2

Where Did We Come From?

Any discussion of the "origin of life" has to go back to the Genesis account of Creation (Gen 1:1-31) that describes the creative process of the Earth and all things on it, including Mankind. The very first verse declares, "In the beginning, God created the Heavens and the Earth."

As I see it, there are but three choices that every person must choose from regarding his or her beliefs.

A. Creation by Almighty God
B. Creation through Evolution (excluding God)
C. Creation by God through an evolutionary process, over time, since God is eternal and has no time constraints.

The Evolutionist theories go something like this: Life began by some "Life Form" that came from the sea. **Hold It! What sea?** There had to be an Earth there for it to be covered with a sea, right? So, where did that Earth and that sea come from? Oh, I get it. It came from the **nothing** caused by the "Big Bang." Anyway, It crawled upon the beach, sprouted arms and legs, and over eons of time, evolved into life as we know it today with people, plants and animals. Of course, the Earth evolved simultaneously with the people, who came from primates, who came from those little "life forms." Later, a branch of the primates developed "brains and skills" that the rest of the primates did not possess; thus, we have today's, Modern Man.

That theory raises some fascinating questions such as, What are Life Forms? Where did they come from? From the sea? What created them, since everything has a beginning, does it not?

By the way, we are still trying to find a primate who is currently in the evolutionary process of becoming a man (even a Neanderthal man). Shouldn't there be a link somewhere.? DUH!

I find it astounding that many highly-educated men and women of science believe this absurd, preposterous theory. Perhaps science and technology have become their god(s) To believe in God means giving up some of their pride and arrogance and, of course, control. Many other scientists believe, as I do, that Almighty God created the universe, Earth, and man. We do not hold that the Earth was created in six literal days, but in God's own time, whatever that may have been because God is eternal and with God time does not exist.

> "He has made everything beautiful in its time; also, he has put eternity in their hearts, except that no one can find out the work that God does from beginning to end." Eccl 3:11

God, who is perfect in all of His ways, and possesses perfect intelligence and creativity created this world in all of its beauty and complexity for His own pleasure, and secondly for all people to enjoy. God, the Bible tells us, created man in His own image and breathed upon him the breath of life and man became a living soul. Man is much more than just another animal. He is of inestimable value to God and is comprised of a body, a spirit, and a soul.

One of the huge differences between man and an animal is the fact that man has an incredibly complex brain. A brain that can plan, reason, calculate, design, invent, relate, memorize, and is the seat of man's emotions. An animal, of course, also has a brain and can perform many of these functions on a limited basis, but operates mainly upon instincts, imbued by the Creator. We all know that certain animals can be highly trained to do certain things and to obey their masters. Animals are taught to perform amazing things, but this is accomplished through repetition and a reward system. Interestingly, though, animals do exhibit emotions, such as fear, sadness, joy, guilt, etc.

In Chapter One, we endeavored to proclaim the greatness of our Creator / God and to describe His awesome creation and the marvelous provisions He has made for our survival, nourishment, material needs, and endless resources for our welfare and enjoyment. All of this preparation was for the purpose of, and for the use of, His crowning creation, Man. Repeating what the Bible says regarding man, "God created man in His own image, breathed upon him the breath of life, and man became a living soul." This body that God gave us is nothing short of numerous miracles! Our bodies are unbelievably complex and awesome, so awesome that only the power, creativity, and intelligence of a Master Designer could have created us.

"Fearfully and Wonderfully Made."

We describe here a few of the systems in our bodies that comprise a human body. Are you ready?

Skeletal Frame:

Supports all internal organs and systems and enables us to walk, run, perform acrobatic moves, dance, play instruments and generally do amazing things with our bodies, e.g., Brain Surgeon, Concert Pianist

Muscular System:

Works in conjunction with our Skeletal System and allows us to have strength and power to do great things.

Coronary System: (Heart)

Our amazing Heart starts pulsating at a rate of 60 -100 beats per minute in about six weeks into pregnancy and beats without stopping until death 70- 90 years later, or longer. I find it incredible that the heart starts beating automatically, without any outside influence or manipulation. The heart delivers nutrients and oxygen to all cells in the body. The arteries carry the blood away from the heart, while the veins carry it back to the heart.

Respiratory System: (Lungs)

Our Lungs provide oxygen to our heart and bloodstream, without which we would die within minutes. They too, start working before we are born and never stop until death.

Digestive System:

Our amazing Stomach and Intestines convert our food into many nutrients that our bodies require. How and where these nutrients are distributed to the various organs, I profess ignorance. We all love good food, don't we?

We do need to be more aware of what we put into our bodies that may be harmful or may contribute to diseases. Also, remember that "Our bodies are the temple of the Holy Spirit."

Nervous System:

Our bodies are "wired" with millions of nerves, which are miraculously connected to our brains. Nerves are comprised of an incredible network of sensory elements that instinctively send messages to the brain. They are, essentially, our **"Five Senses" Sight, Hearing, Tasting, Smelling, and Touch**

When we are injured, to the slightest degree, or develop some sickness or disease, we feel pain, and that pain signal is transmitted to the brain to alert the brain that there is a problem or abnormality. Conversely, if the brain, which is the seat of our emotions, allows negativity, such as fear, anxiety, hatred, etc. to dominate our thinking, the nervous system can be adversely affected and even become debilitating.

There are, of course, many more organs and systems in our bodies, all of which are vitally important, and whose functions are critical to our survival and well-being. All of these vital functions work, in unison, twenty-four hours a day, seven days a week. If just one of these ceases to function, we face a serious medical situation, and potentially death. So, thank God for your good health and for dedicated doctors, nurses and care providers.

Most importantly, thank God, who invites us to come to Him in prayer for all of our needs, as well as for healing. Sometimes God heals directly and instantaneously, sometimes through modern medicine and physicians. Additionally, God made our bodies to be "self-healing" to a certain degree, e.g., cuts and bruises.

"Our Miraculous Five Senses"

Sight:

<u>Think about it!</u> The miracle of **Sight**. The anatomy of the eye is nothing short of incredible. The eye has many components, including the cornea, iris, pupil, lens, retina, macula, optic nerve, choroid, and vitreous. The cornea transmits and focuses light into the eye. The light projects through the pupil and lens to the back of the eye. The inside lining of the eye is covered by special light-sensing cells that comprise the retina. It converts light into electrical impulses. Behind the eye, the optic nerve carries these impulses to the brain. What a blessing that we are permitted to see and enjoy the fantastic beauty of God's rich creation; the majestic mountains, the cascading streams, the lakes, the forests, the fluffy white clouds in azure blue skies, the beautiful flowers, the colorful songbirds, and, of course, our loved ones.

Dr. Werner Von Braun, Rocket Scientist, made this statement, "To believe only one conclusion—that everything in the universe happened by chance would violate the very objectivity of science itself. What random process could produce the brains of a man, or the system of the human eye."

Hearing:

The miracle of **Hearing** is another of our God-given gifts. Like the human eye, the human ear is miraculous. Sound waves travel from the outer ear and in through the auditory canal, causing the eardrum (tympanic membrane) to vibrate. The vibrations move through the oval window through the fluid in the cochlea in the inner ear, stimulating thousands of tiny hair cells. Other components include the eardrum, hammer, anvil, stirrup, eustachian tube, cochlea, and auditory nerves. Through this amazing auditory system, sounds are transmitted to the brain.

How great it is that we can communicate with each other and understand and relate to each other. Our amazing ears can not only warn us of impending danger but can also allow us to enjoy great music, the music of nature, the sounds of children playing, a beautiful sonata, the sounds of Christmas and on and on.

Taste:

Everyone loves good food, which is why we have the sense of **Taste**, an amazing gift that enables us to identify the foods we enjoy the most. Our tongues have "Sensors" called "Taste Buds" that determine what we like and what we do not like. What if everything we ate was bland and boring?

Fortunately, our Creator provided all good things for us to enjoy.

Smell:

The next of the "five senses" is the sense of **Smell.** The smell of some foods set our taste buds on fire. The smell of a sizzling rib-eye steak, smothered with onions can make a hungry man drool. Also, certain odors can bring back memories of past times or events, particularly if they were pleasant times. Humans detect smells by inhaling air that contains odor molecules, which then bind to receptors inside the nose, relaying messages to the brain. Studies show that the human nose can easily detect in excess of 10,000 distinct smells. Our noses are necessary breathing passages and serve as air filters as well.

Touch:

Lastly, the final sense is the sense of **Touch.** Our sense of touch is truly an incredibly sensitive gift. It is difficult to put into words all that is wrapped up within this phenomenon. A touch can be gentle, or it can be rough.

We all know that a touch, at the right time, and in the right way, can have a tremendous, positive effect on another person. Our fingertips are so sensitive that the most minute particles can be detected across a very smooth surface. Blind people tend to have the most sensitive touch since they are capable of reading Braille and navigating around by themselves

In his book, "Touch, the Science of Hand, Heart, and Mind," Dr. David Linden, regarding touching in childhood, states, "Touch is not optional for human development. We have the longest childhoods of any animal. There is no other creature whose five-year-old offspring cannot live independently.If our long childhoods are not filled with touch, particularly loving, inter-personal touch, the consequences are dramatic."

All of the senses mentioned above, and many

more, send electronic impulses to the brain which processes these impulses at an unbelievable speed. Many studies reveal that our brains can store 100 million facts, and can handle 15,000 decisions per second.

In summary, our physical bodies, with all of its complex systems, and our five incredible senses, all working together, in unison, compel us to honor and praise our Creator God, the only one with the power, the creativity, and the intelligence to do the impossible, made us in His own image, and who sustains us.

"Your DNA is WOW"

Most amazing of all is this! There has never been, and never will be, anybody exactly like YOU. Here is the scientific description of the term DNA (deoxyribonucleic acid) per dictionary.com "A nucleic acid that consists of two long chains of Nucleotides twisted together into a double helix, and joined by hydrogen bonds between complementary bases Adenine and Thiamine or Cytosine and Guanine." The DNA carries the cell's genetic information and hereditary characteristics via its Nucleotides.

Every person and nearly other thing on Earth has a DNA which the Creator placed in them that makes each individual totally unique and very special.

That, my friend, tells me that you and I, and every other human on Earth, are special and precious in God's sight! We are ONE OF A KIND!

The reliability of the DNA "footprint" has replaced the "fingerprint" when it comes to identifying any individual. Several prison inmates have recently been set free due to DNA evidence proving their innocence.

Recently, I "pulled up" my bank account on my "smartphone" to access my account. An automated "voice" directed me to say the following words: "My voice is my password, please verify me." We all know that bankers are not the most trusting people in the world, right? Amazingly, our voices are so unique that they serve to positively identify every individual, among the tens of thousands of customers.

Who else, or what else, could have made Heaven and Earth and Us?

Chapter 3

Animal Instincts

We discussed, very briefly, in the previous chapter, the basic differences between animals and man. Man, of course, was created in the image of God, and given dominion over all animals on the Earth, and possesses an extremely complex brain and a strong sense of morality. Animals, however, operate mainly on God-infused instincts.

Some of the interesting facts regarding animals that I find fascinating are as follows:

Firstly, to ensure the continuing existence of each species, the Creator equipped each animal with either a means of defense or a means of escape or concealment. (camouflage) i.e., a deer fawn's coloration and spots make detection very unlikely while lying in foliage.

In nature, there exists a balance between predator and prey. Even though some prey appear to be very vulnerable, enough of the species will survive to ensure the preservation of the species. Eventually, in many cases, the predator is devoured by another larger and more powerful predator. Even though it may seem unfair that the predator has a tremendous advantage over a smaller animal, a predator often goes hungry for days until it is finally successful. This is because the prey, such as a gazelle, or impala or some other fleet-footed animal with superior sight and hearing can see and hear the predator approaching and can simply out-run the predator.

"Home Sweet Home"

An amazing instinct known as "The Homing Instinct" is inherent in many animals, birds, and fish.

A prime example is the Salmon. Hatched from eggs in a remote mountain stream, they swim downstream for miles to reach the open ocean, The salmon grow and flourish in the ocean miles and miles from their birthplace and, inexplicably, return to the exact stream where they were born, then swim upstream, against almost impossible odds to their spawning areas only to lay their eggs and die. Of course, one of the chief beneficiaries of this phenomenon happens to be the bears, who gorge themselves with salmon in preparation for their winter hibernation.

Let's look at Wild Geese and their homing

instincts. From their homeland in the Canadian wild, they sense cold weather coming, and the need to go south. So, the "Lead Goose" in the goose hierarchy decides one day, it's time, and off they go. They instinctively know the right direction and fly in a "V" formation to the southern United States and beyond. The "V" formation allows each trailing goose to benefit from the wash of air from the wings of the goose in front and so on, from front to rear. (so, it is not by chance). conversely, the opposite is true when the geese decide it is time to head back home up north.

A similar scenario exists regarding birds. You, no doubt, have heard about the Swallows, who, at a specific time, leave their normal location and head for Capistrano. There they stay until the day they begin their return flight. Do these creatures have some internal time clock that tells them when to go and when to return?

Butterflies are creatures that we all are familiar with and are amazed at their beauty and grace. The life cycle of butterflies is truly unbelievable. The female, having mated with a male, lays her eggs usually on the underside of a leaf, to protect them from sunlight and rain. After bursting out of the eggshell, the caterpillar gorges on leaves and then eats the shell. As they grow, the caterpillar sheds it's skin several times. When fully grown, the caterpillar finds a place to "pupate." It then spins a small silk pad to which it attaches its tail and from which it suspends itself, hanging upside down. It sheds its last skin and becomes a "pupa." Inside the pupa, a transformation starts taking place called a metamorphosis, and the lowly caterpillar is transformed into a beautiful butterfly!

The colors and patterns of butterflies' wings are vivid and beautiful and always perfectly symmetrical. Many species of butterflies migrate elsewhere, such as the Monarch migration, by instinct.

> "Therefore, if anyone is in Christ, he is a New Creation; Old things have passed away; behold, all things have Become new" 2 Corinthians 5-17

Consider the amazing little Hummingbird, the smallest of birds. Although small, their brain makes up a whopping 4.2 percent of their weight (the largest of any bird). Studies have shown that hummingbirds can remember every flower they have ever visited and even recognize humans and know which ones will refill their feeders. They have great vision and can see every color that we can. Hummingbird males can get mean during mating season and can attack the competition. They can fly forward, backward, upside down, sideways and also hover. Hummingbirds beat their wings at the incredible speed of 70 to 200 times per second. **(That's Per Second)**

Like all created animals and birds, these hummingbirds are arrayed in vivid colors and patterns that no evolutionary process could ever hope to duplicate.

Many animals possess instincts that use a type of "logic," especially when hunting. Wolves, hyenas, and lions come to mind. They seem to work together for the common purpose of trapping their prey. Killer whales (Orcas) do this. In pursuing a large spread of Krill, they keep circling the krill, intimidating them, and forcing them to form a tight ball. Then they attack, scooping them up by the dozens. They also use intimidation tactics on sea lion pups, circling and splashing until the pups get confused, frightened, and go into the water to their demise.

"Eeewww! Bugs!!"

No one likes insects, right? Yes, but they are part of creation and have a purpose. Ants, wasps, hornets, bees, and dirt daubers all have functions, many of which we do not understand. Of them all, bees are the insects we favor, because they provide what we want, namely Honey. Insects seem to be "Goal-Driven" the goal being constantly eating, reproducing, and serving the Queen. There is definitely a social order to these insects, which include "workers" and "soldiers," among other things. They are not lazy and work from dawn to dusk.

One of the most incredible insects, in my opinion, is the spider. The spider is a planner, devising, and building a web to trap food. Equipped with a reservoir of silk thread, the spider dives or jumps from one point to another, to create one thread to work with. It then begins to create radial strands of webbing, spacing them apart at precisely the same distance from each other. Then the spider starts lateral webbing, spacing the strands at precisely the same distance apart from each other. When the web is done, the spider parks at one end and waits for a bug or a fly to be caught in the web, and quickly winds it up with silk for future consumption. How and where did the spider obtain its silk.? And where did the knowledge to create a web in a precise pattern come from.?

While many animals and other creatures in the wild are harmless and avoid human contact, there are, obviously, many more that are to be avoided at all costs, to mention a few: bears, hyenas, wild dogs, snakes, and the big cat family (lions, tigers, leopards, panthers, jaguars, and cheetahs). Never provoke a wild animal, even if the animal doesn't seem to be in the attack mode.

Once, as a young boy, I saw a large water moccasin lying on a sand bar across a narrow creek. I thought it would be fun to throw rocks at the snake and see his reaction. After some near-misses, one of my rocks hit the snake, and it started immediately slithering after me! Scared, my heart pounding, I ran as fast as I could until I was sure the danger was over!

"Attitudes Concerning Animals."

Many people are so caught up in the "rat race" of life, expending their time and energy in the pursuit of power, status and money, that they fail to appreciate the really important things in life, such as God, family, and the natural world. We work long and hard to earn money to buy the things we do not need.

The wealthy **Big Game Hunter** sees animals as nothing more than another "trophy" to mount on the wall in his mansion. A safari is, basically, an "ego trip," many times under the guise of conservatism. So what, if he hires an entourage of a dozen men with guns (in case he misses, or the animal charges) or that he uses "High Tech" equipment to ensure that he is successful in killing an animal for fun.

The **Poacher**, on the other hand, sees animals as easy money and has no regard for the law or the defenseless animal. These types of people are truly the "low life" specimens of humanity.

The **Conservationist** sees all wildlife as potentially endangered species, and are almost militant in their zeal to protect them. Some of the most zealous of these individuals seem more interested in saving endangered species than saving human babies, which **are truly endangered**.

With the exception of dogs and cats, the average person in our society is only mildly interested in animals and prefers to see them only occasionally In a zoo, and in their cages. Animals are to be studied, appreciated, and should not be exploited, or made to look ridiculous. Obviously, the natural habitat of all animals should be protected. There are several TV networks, such as National Geographic Channel, that carry excellent nature programming that cover the Earth itself, the plant and animal kingdoms, and much more. Also, the photography and narratives are fantastic.

I was recently reminded why I dislike zoos so much. When I visited a zoo in Florida, one of the animals exhibited there was a Cheetah, a beautiful animal that is believed to be the fastest animal in the world. The cheetah's "home" was an area of about 300 square feet, surrounded by a chain-link fence (sides and roof) that attempted to simulate the animal's "natural environment." This so-called environment was woefully inadequate, and I was saddened to see such a magnificent animal, who was "born free," caged up in this manner.

You have, probably, seen the movie entitled "Hatari," starring John Wayne and Red Buttons, made in 1962. It was an entertaining, action movie in many ways, as John Wayne movies usually are.

The movie was interspersed with comedy and romance, which were all good. John Wayne's sole business, however, was capturing wild animals in Africa, and selling them to zoos in many countries, including everything from monkeys to rhinos. We are to have dominion over animals, as the Bible states, as a food source, when needed, but also to train and use animals to help us accomplish work tasks and services. We are not to exploit animals for money.

> "Be fruitful and fill the Earth and subdue it and have dominion over the fish of the sea the Birds of the air, and over every living thing that moves upon the Earth." Gen 1:28

Chapter 4

Symmetry and Color in Nature

One of the wonders of creation, which is prevalent in nearly all creatures is the characteristic of symmetry. Nowhere else can we begin to comprehend the intelligence and creative genius of our God. The Master Painter blends the symmetry of all humans, animals, insects, reptiles, plants, and flowers with an unbelievable array of colors and textures.

Symmetry exists in not only the "mirror image" form that we are all familiar with but in several other forms such as circular, linear, and radial. Classic examples of "mirror image" symmetry are these butterflies depicted on the back cover of this book.

Being a designer myself, I know that symmetry is important in design. We want things to be balanced and not off-center. Symmetry gives us a sense of "rightness" so that objects "look right" and "feel right." Also, from a functional or physical standpoint, only symmetry makes sense. Our eyes, noses, ears, lips, arms, and legs are perfectly symmetrical and in the right places to not only look right but to look great and to perform all functions well.

Consider Snowflakes, which are actually drops of water that crystalize during their descent from the sky. Snowflakes form an amazing array of symmetrical shapes and forms, and while it may be impossible to prove, it has been said that no two snowflakes are exactly alike. The forming of snowflakes serve as another example of matter, changing from a liquid to a solid, but still remaining H_2O (water).

If I may take a little side trip and extol the aesthetic beauty of snow; Have you ever had the awesome experience of walking on a carpet of freshly fallen snow, through a stand of Aspens on a bright sunny morning? Beautiful and Peaceful! With sunlight filtering through the shimmering golden aspen leaves, the feeling is almost "magical!"

Another type of symmetry is "Radial" symmetry. If one drops a rock into a body of water, the waves created, radiate in a circular pattern, each wave creating the successive wave and so on, until the energy created finally dissipates.

So, we see clearly, that the Creator loved the order, beauty, and logic of symmetry in the creative process, not only in humankind, and animals but in numerous elements of creation.

Chapter 5

Timing is Everything.

Years back, I invented, and applied for U.S.Patents for the following inventions and systems:

1. A pre-packaged, charcoal foil-wrapped, fuel-ready method for barbecue grilles, whereby the user peels back the top folds of foil, lights the coals and is ready to grill. When done, folds the spent container up and disposes of the ashes, leaving the grill clean and neat.

RESULT: Too Late!! Someone else beat me to it!

2. The Brake Light in the rear window of every automobile made in the USA since the year 1986 required by law. My invention was deemed similar but did not have enough unique features to win the patent. This,

of course, would have made me a very rich man.

RESULT: Too Late!! (But not by much) Should have acted sooner!!

3. An Avalanche Survival System: Designed to keep a person buried underneath a snow avalanche alive for at least 60 minutes, while searchers locate and rescue the buried person. The device had other features that aided in locating the victim.

RESULT: SUCCESS! This time, I was granted a U.S. Patent

Although for God, time does not exist, He gave us the blessing of time, through creation. As explained in Chapter 1, The vast universe, created by God operates on incredibly precise timing. Further, the rotations of the Earth, sun, and moon are what we base our system of time on, and what creates the rhythm of life that we are used to. Without a precise system of time, our homes, our government, our institutions, our world, would be in total chaos.

The Bible is God's word and our "owner's manual" for life. In it, His word talks about time and the various events of life as relates to time.

"To everything, there is a season.
A time for every purpose under
Heaven".

A time to be born, and a time to die.
A time to plant, and a time to pluck
what is planted.
A time to kill, and a time to heal.
A time to break down, and a time to
build up.
A time to weep, and a time to laugh.
A time to mourn, and a time to dance.
A time to cast away stones, and a
time to gather stones.
A time to embrace, and a time to
refrain from embracing.
A time to gain, and a time to lose.
A time to keep, and a time to throw
away.
A time to tear, and a time to sew.
A time to keep silence, and a time to
speak.
A time to love, and a time to hate.
A time of war, and a time of peace
Eccl: 3:1-8

If you live in Colorado, there's also a time for
deer hunting! My son and I have been on several
deer/elk hunts. These hunts are really all about

bonding and enjoying the great outdoors together. But, on this one hunt,

I positioned myself, lying down in some fairly high grass and waited for the deer to come by. We could hear them coming from behind some large rock formations, and I anticipated taking my shot as they emerged from the rocks. The deer nearest me stopped for about one second and kept on going. It was getting dark, and I wasn't sure it was a legal buck, so I paused. I reasoned that the deer would all stop at the edge of the stream there to drink, and that's when I would have a perfect shot. To my surprise and amazement, the deer just kept on going through the water and disappeared from view. Talk about bad timing!

Back to the timing issue, If you're an NFL fan, you know that all the teams have a few "trick plays" in their back pockets. For example, there is the "Fake Punt," the "Fake Field Goal" try, the "Halfback Pass" and the "Flea Flicker." When called at precisely the right time, these trick plays are often successful and can even be game-winners! But to succeed, the timing and the execution has to be perfect.

Just as everything in creation has a purpose, You and I also have a purpose! We are not just walking around on this Earth, occupying space, and being jerked around or bounced around from place to place and circumstance to circumstance, like the ball in a pinball machine.

Our 'Number One" purpose is to love and glorify God, and to find His will for our lives and to obey His will. If we seek His will, it is God's responsibility to reveal it. It is our responsibility to obey and endeavor to do it, as He leads. You may be thinking, "I don't know if I have enough faith to trust Jesus as my Saviour and to believe the Bible. After all, science has some pretty strong arguments about creation and the origin of man and all."

We all have been given the capacity to believe in our Creator. We all have faith in many things, even in things over which we have no control. When we are driving down a two-lane highway at, say 65 miles per hour, and someone else's vehicle is heading toward us in the opposite lane also, perhaps, at a speed of 65 miles per hour, we are confident that our vehicle will be in the center of our lane because we are in control. We are not, however, sure that the driver of that vehicle is in control of their car. He or she could be drifting off to sleep, or high on drugs, or distracted to the point that they lose control, or the lights of your car may be blinding them, We all find ourselves in this situation perhaps hundreds of times each day, but that doesn't stop us from driving our cars, does it?

When we turn on the light switches in our homes, we have faith that the lights will come on, even though we don't really understand electricity.

We do not have to understand electricity to utilize it and to benefit from it.

When we board that huge "Aluminum Tube with Wings," and they close the door, our faith is basically in two (2) human beings, the Pilot and the Co-Pilot! We also are depending upon the mechanics and service people as well. We base our faith on the fact that these people are reliable and well - trained, don't we? We read about airliners crashing, wiping out hundreds of people at a time, but that doesn't stop us from traveling by air, because we figure the odds are in our favor, right?

Think about LIGHT for a moment. What is it, exactly? A simple question, but very difficult to answer. In his book entitled "The Reason Why Faith Makes Sense," Mark Mittelberg says "If scientists are still trying to define and explain the nature of light, then why do we believe it exists at all? Because we see it, or perhaps more accurately, we see with it. Either way, we don't have to fully grasp what light is in order to believe in it. Similarly, although we can't fully define God, we can know that He exists because we can see the manifestation of Him everywhere around us."

I base my faith upon the actual Creator of the Universe who created all things and all people, came to Earth and dwelt among us, died on a cross to save us from the penalty of sin, and gave to us the gift of Eternal Life. That's who my faith is in!

He has made everything beautiful in its time, also, he has put eternity in their hearts, except that no one can find out the work that God does from beginning". Eccl 3:11

Chapter 6

The Nature of Nature:

Every person and everything in nature was created by God and has a purpose and an individual DNA. Everything **takes from** nature and **gives back** to nature.

For example, a tree takes nutrients from the soil, water from the rain, photosynthesis from the Sunlight, and oxygen from the air. The tree **gives back** shade, fruit or whatever, oxygen, soil stabilization, a habitat for many types of creatures, seedlings for new growth, color, and beauty.

We, as creatures of God, are the blessed beneficiaries of His awesome creation and all of its bounty! We gladly take from all that the Creator provides, but what do we give back in return. I believe our responses to God's amazing love and generosity should be:

> ➢ Our complete love, devotion, and service
> ➢ Unending gratitude and praise
> ➢ Love and respect for all life!
> ➢ Respect for, and preservation of, our Earth and all of creation
> ➢ Serve and help those in need, as for the Lord
> ➢ Promote Peace and Unity in our society

Natural Disasters:

Contrary to what some believe, the Earth is not static but dynamic, and in a constant state of motion. Pick up a rock. It is heavy, it looks and feels solid, and it certainly is not moving, right? Wrong! It is moving. Rock, like everything else, is "matter," the basic unit of matter is the atom. Atoms are comprised of a nucleus of Protons and Neutrons and of Electrons which rotate around the nucleus. Atoms combine to form Molecules, that interact to form solids, liquids or gases, in this case, a solid. However, over eons of time, rocks can change from one type to another type and back, depending upon the forces acting upon them, such as intense heat and pressure.

While we do not feel the movement of the Earth, it is spinning around its axis at the rate of 1,037 MPH. Simultaneously, it is traveling in an orbit around the sun at 67,000 MPH. It takes one year to completely orbit the sun, which is the factor that produces our four seasons.

Additionally, there are vast "Tectonic Plates" underneath the surface of the Earth that are in constant, but ever so slow, motion. The shifting of these plates can cause fissures in the mantle of the Earth's crust through which molten lava can travel upward, under pressure, resulting in volcanic eruptions.

Faults in the Earth's crust can cause earthquakes. Sometimes large masses of earth break off and fall into the ocean, thereby causing Tsunamis, which, of course, can be devastating. All of these occurrences, along with floods, tornadoes, forest fires, etc., are natural disasters which were brought about by the fall of man, when man rebelled against God in the beginning. As a result, the Earth is a very dangerous place! It is, at the same time, the most beautiful, most plentiful, most marvelous place in this universe.

The Earth is self-sustaining in that all plants, animals, birds, fish, reptiles and all other creatures reproduce their own kind, keeping their individual species alive. (with a few exceptions). We have seen actual photographs and videos, taken by Hubbell, of the moon, Mars, Venus, and other planets. In each case, the surfaces of these planets and the moon, are barren, stark, crater-ridden, desolate, colorless landscapes and present an atmosphere in which the human body is not designed to function. **We were made for Earth! Earth was made for us!!**

According to Wikipedia, the challenges that face humankind in its attempt to travel to Mars, and to establish a colony there include the following formidable, logistical, physical and psychological obstacles:

Radiation Which can double the DOE limit of .66 Sieverts as reported by a NASA report on September 2017, due to a massive unexpected solar storm. This indicates, to me, that radiation levels are subject to unpredictable weather conditions.

Weightlessness: Prolonged weightlessness can harm the body.

Eyesight Impairment: Possible adverse effect due to prolonged weightlessness.

Psychological Effects: Due to isolation, lack of community, lack of real-time connection with Earth

Social Effects: Cramped conditions for up to 2 or 3 years

Medical Care: Lack of Medical facilities, en route, and on the surface

Potential Malfunctions: Possible failure of propulsion systems or support equipment

Lack of Fuel: Possible lack of fuel for a round trip. May be forced to make fuel from Methane and Oxygen (if that is possible).

Contamination: Possible contamination of Mars and Earth due to human microbiota.

Additionally, other countries have joined this race to Mars, including Japan, China, Russia, and

India. All have space programs. NASA is under presidential orders to land humans on Mars by 2033

Why humankind is determined to sacrifice hundreds of lives, trillions of our dollars and blow our natural resources to reach **"the unreachable star"** is beyond me! Where is the reward, the great payday?

As mentioned in Chapter 1, The logistics of such an endeavor, the cost in human lives, and the enormous financial investment are totally impractical with little or no benefits to humankind.

Imagine, for a moment, that you are among the first group of visitors to Mars. As you wander around on the Martian surface, in your space suit with a glass bubble helmet, (the air is 100 times thinner than Earth's air and is mostly CO_2), you will probably start asking yourself the following questions:

Where are the trees? Where are the rivers and lakes?

Where are the blue skies and white clouds, instead of a brownish-red sky?

Where are the birds, the flowers, the animals?

Where are the people? Where are the restroom facilities?

Where are the cars? Where are the taxi-cabs?

Where are the hotels and restaurants? Where is McDonalds?

Where is my winter coat? (The temperature is, on the average -80 degrees Fahrenheit. That is **80 degrees below zero, and can get down to minus 195 degrees below zero!**

How can they play football and baseball in this kind of stupid weather, and in this crazy gravity?

Where are the beaches and the mountains?

The most urgent question in your mind, at this point, is how soon can I get back to Earth? Well, realistically, the next "window of opportunity" when the Earth is closest to Mars, could be 26 months, and the trip home another 6 to 9 months, so possibly around two years and 11 months, if all goes well. Meanwhile, enjoy your stay in the land of promise, where humankind can start afresh!

Be reminded that we are so blessed to be living on this awesome, amazing, magnificent Earth, our exclusive "Home In Space" like no other in this vast universe. In reality, you and I, and everyone living today will be "long gone," if and when, humankind inhabits a distant planet. We will have received our reward,

Eternal Life with our Creator God in Heaven with all the Redeemed!!

Chapter 7

"Blue Skies Ahead"

I am a licensed Private Pilot, although I haven't flown an aircraft for many years. When I was a student pilot, an important phase of my flight training was "cross country" flying. My first solo cross-country flight was filled with anxiety for fear of getting lost and forgetting important procedures and facts.

Thankfully, I made it back to the field safely. I found out that if I applied the knowledge that my Instructor had taught me, there was nothing to fear, and I could relax and enjoy flying.

Flying by VFR (visual flight rules) means that the pilot uses his eyes for nearly everything in controlling the aircraft. He uses aeronautical charts to plot his course and to identify checkpoints below as he flies his plotted course and is in contact with control zones and airport control towers (this was "way back when"). There are certain principles and procedures involved in VFR cross-country flying, and in life applications as well.

Here are a few of those guidelines:

Destination:

Before you start out, you must have a specific destination in mind.

If you wish to fly to Denver, you don't head for New Orleans. Likewise, if Heaven is your destination when you depart from this Earth, there is a sure course to get you there. It's called the Bible!

Set Your Course:

Plot your course by Bible Study / Prayer / Belief

Checkpoints:

Do spiritual checkpoints along the way to ensure that you are still on course.

Deviations:

Deal with deviations as they occur. (drifting off course) (swirling winds of doctrine)

Weather:

There may be sudden unexpected conditions. Stay alert and skirt around those ominous signs.

Communications:

Always keep in constant communication with the Control Authority (GOD) Listen for Advisories. Avoid negative traffic in your flight path.

Approach:

Approach the Control Authority with confidence, but obey landing instructions.

Landing:

Wheels down, flaps down, throttle back! Glide on in for a Perfect landing!

You know, unless you're a famous personality, athlete, or movie star, your arrival at the airport probably doesn't generate a lot of excitement except for a few friends and family, right?

Your arrival in Heaven, however, will be a completely different story! It will be the **absolute best day of your life!** It will be a day of hilarious rejoicing, dancing and singing, with millions of angels all around, joining in the celebration. That's when you may stand, face to face, with your Lord and Savior, Jesus Christ, and behold His glory!

This is the Ultimate flight......FLIGHT FINAL. This is the Ultimate DESTINATION!

Chapter 8

The Way

Jesus, the Creator, said, " I am the Way, the Truth and the Life. No man cometh to the Father, except through me." John 14:6

What, exactly, is the WAY? It is simply believing that Jesus is the Son of God, who died on the cross, took upon Himself our sins, and offers forgiveness and the gift of eternal life to all who believe. It is confessing our sins and trusting Jesus as Saviour and Lord. It is following Jesus, day by day.

"Choose you, this day, whom you will serve."

The great thing about God is that He gave us the options to choose our Earthly paths and our eternal destiny. The Creator gave every one of us the right to choose good or evil, God or satan,

Heaven or Hell. (I purposely did not capitalize his name, as that would be honoring the evil one).

We have already described the extent that God went to in order to show His love for every one of His creatures, and His desire to be in an intimate relationship with us in the present and throughout eternity, but since He endowed us with the gift of free moral agency, we must choose whom we are going to follow. We really can't remain neutral. We must make a conscious decision

There is an endless variety of distractions (excuses) that prevent or delay people from making a decision to follow Jesus. Some of these are pride, doubts, and fears of all kinds. Where do these distractions originate? They originate from satan himself! The Bible describes satan as "Destroyer," "Deceiver," "Liar," and the "Father of Liars."

When the choices have been so clearly defined, the decision to accept Jesus Christ should be a "no brainer" "Sure, I choose good over evil." "Sure, I choose morality over immorality." "Sure, I absolutely choose Heaven over Hell."

The problems are issues such as pride, doubts, and fears that permeate our minds, along with the pressures of our society, prevent us from making a decision for Christ. Additionally, we have bought into the ideas that money, status, nice homes, cars, and "toys" will satisfy all of our heart's desires. While these things are all good, they cannot fill the gap between our Creator and us.

By default, a man is the spiritual leader of his house. This is the way God established the family unit. What do we really value the most, relationships or things? The relentless pursuit of material things, at the expense of a man's family, is a tragic mistake. As men, we need to "man-up" and get our priorities in line. i.e., God, family, church, and work. The easy way is to "go with the flow," don't rock the boat." Jesus tells us, "Be not conformed to this world, but be transformed by the renewing of your mind."

I see some parallels between the laws of nature and the laws of God. For example, in nature, everything must die to re-generate (to live again.) I am not talking about re-incarnation. If a forest burns and dies, it will eventually be re-created by new life, and become even more healthy because of the enriched soil provided by the decayed trees.

In the spiritual realm, we humans are no exception. We must "die to sin" (be saved) in order to become a "New Creature" in Christ. When we die, physically, if we have been saved, we will be resurrected when Christ comes again and will receive the gift of Eternal Life.

To emphasize this truth, the Bible says that we won't just have eternal life when we die, but if we are in Christ, we already have it.

> "For this is the testimony that God
> has given us eternal life, and this

> life is in His Son. He who has the Son has life; He who does not have the Son of God does not have life." 1 John 5:12

What about Church?

Do I have to go to church to be a Christian? The answer to that is NO! However, there are many good reasons why you should be part of a dynamic, growing, spiritual body of believers.

First off, we weren't meant to make this life journey all alone. We need the support, fellowship, encouragement, and the preached Word to guide and to empower us. We are saved by faith, not works, but we choose to serve, to give, to participate, and to share our experiences with others for their encouragement. There is power in corporate worship. There is power in the preached Word of God. There is power and inspiration in singing the songs of praise and worship together.

Additionally, the church, through dedicated members, and sheer numbers, can accomplish amazing things, world-wide, that could not be done otherwise.

"Yeah, but aren't there a bunch of hypocrites in churches? " Yes, there are, but you cannot allow a few hypocrites to keep you out of the Kingdom.

God will deal with them, and maybe you will be a positive influence for them by your example.

"Yeah, but won't being a Christian take away all my fun? " No, on the contrary, the Christian life is exciting and liberating in that there is freedom from guilt of the past, and anxiety over the future. As a New Creature in Christ Jesus, you will have a new outlook on life, and a new set of values. You will have a purpose and a calling to fulfill.

Get On Board!

There are many religions, cults, false doctrines, and false teachers out there in our world. The Bible warns us about these things and urges us to beware of such. The Bible has stood the test of time in spite of thousands of years of "bible bashing." No one has been able to find any contradictions of any kind. It remains the **"Infallible Word of God."** "In God, We Trust" is still printed on our money. "One Nation, under God" is still in our Pledge of Allegiance.

Our Founding Fathers and many other prominent figures in our history publicly declared their belief in the Bible.

Here are a few:

George Washington, Founder of our Nation
Andrew Jackson, Former President of the United States

Theodore Roosevelt, Former President of the United States

Winston Churchill, Prime Minister of England

Ronald Reagan, Former President of the United States

Robert E. Lee, General

Franklin D. Roosevelt, Former President of the United States

Patrick Henry, Patriot

William McKinley, Former President of the United States

Thomas Jefferson, Former President of the United States

Samuel Morse, Inventor of the Telegraph

Christopher Columbus, Discoverer of the New World

Dwight Eisenhower, Former President of the United States

Calvin Coolidge, Former President of the United States

John Adams, Former President of the United States

Ulysses S. Grant, Former President of the United States

John Quincy Adams, Former President of the United States

Abraham Lincoln, Former President of the United States

Dr. Wernher Von Braun, Rocket Scientist, Physicist

Margaret Thatcher, former Prime Minister of England

Were these men and women illiterate, uneducated yokels? No, these persons were some of the world's most educated, brilliant-minded people, and were leaders of the greatest nations that the world has ever seen.

"To be forced to believe that everything in the Universe happened by chance would violate the very objectivity of science itself, what random process could produce the brain of a man or the system of the human eye."

"The Bible is the revelation of God's nature and love."

Dr. Wernher Von Braun

"Lives of great men all remind us, we can make our lives sublime, and departing, leave behind us Footprints on the sands of time."
Longfellow

"For the Beauty of the Earth"

> "For the Beauty of the Earth, for the
> glory of the skies, for the love which
> from our birth, over and around us
> lies"

Christ, our Lord, to you we raise this, our hymn of
grateful praise

> "For the wonder of each hour, of the
> day and of the night, hill and dale
> and tree and flower, sun and moon
> and stars of light"

Christ, our Lord, to you we raise this, our hymn of
grateful praise

> ""For the joy of human love, brother,
> sister, parent, child friends on Earth
> and friends above, for all gentle
> thoughts and mild

Christ, our Lord, to you we raise this, our hymn of
grateful praise

> "For yourself, best gift divine, to the
> world so freely given, agent of God's
> grand design. Peace on Earth and
> Joy in Heaven".

Christ, our Lord, to you we raise this, our hymn of grateful praise

Folliott S. Pierpoint
1835-1917

About the Author:

Carl D, Rowe is an Architectural Project Manager, a Custom Home Designer, a former General Contractor, an Amateur Inventor, and a Private Pilot. He is also An avid outdoors person who enjoys camping, hiking, hunting, fishing, golf and all types of adventures.

Mr. Rowe served his country as a veteran of the Korean war as a member of the U. S. Air force. He was formerly active in the Civitan service club, and the Gideons. He earned the Good Conduct Medal, The United Nations Service Medal. The National Defense Service Medal, and The Korean Service Medal with 1 Bronze Star.

Being a Christian for most of his life, Mr. Rowe felt that he needed to share the Gospel in any way he felt lead to do so. One of the ways he chose to do this was through the medium of music and was a member of several church choirs and quartets.

He also felt that there currently exists a great need to reach out to high school and college students, millennials, and to people in general, who may lack knowledge of the Bible and the plan of salvation, and for whatever reason, would never attend a church, but might read a book about God and His marvelous creation, where we came from, how the Christian worldview differs from much of science, and the many reasons why. Most importantly, how our choices determine our eternal destiny.

Mr. Rowe does not claim to be an authority on religion or science and the contents of this book represent his personal beliefs and observations.

Carl and his wife, Virginia, reside in Colorado.

Acknowledgments

Thank You, to my entire family, and my many friends, for your encouragement and support.

Thank You, Holy Spirit, for implanting in my mind the idea and purpose for this book, back in 2015 and for helping me to overcome doubt and discouragement. Thank You for allowing us to build our cabin in the mountains, where the inspiration for this book was conceived.

A big Thanks to Westbow Press for their guidance and editorial assistance along the way, Special thanks to our daughter, Mar'ti Priscilla Thomas for her time, energy and editing skills.

"To God, be all Glory and Praise!"

Discussion Topics:

Chapter 1 "The Earth.... Our Home in Space"

Do you believe that the Earth is the only planet in our vast universe that has human life on it?

How do you interpret John 10:16 " and Other Sheep I have, which are not of this fold; them also I must bring, and they will hear my voice, and there will be One Fold and One Shepherd."

Chapter 2 "Where Did We Come From"

What is the difference between "FACT" and "Theory"?

What are some of the ways that confirm our personal identity, as individuals, and not just another human being?

Chapter 3 "Animal Instincts"

What is an animal's primal instinct?

How would you explain the "Homing Instinct" in animals, fish, birds, and many other creatures?

Having read about the amazing s instincts of these creatures, can you attribute these amazing gifts to an evolutionary process, or were they imbued in all creation by God?

Chapter 4 "Symmetry and Color in Nature"

Take a look at the three Butterflies depicted on the back cover of this book.
What characteristics do you see in these images?

Did you see strong evidence of a Master Designer and of an awesome Artist? Did you realize that this artistry takes place while the Butterfly is going through an amazing metamorphosis and emerges a beautiful creature?

Chapter 5 'Timing is Everything"

We tend to forget that TIME is a creation of man, but made possible by God,s creative acts. What acts of creation made our system of time possible?

In our world today, what makes timing so important?

Chapter 6 "The Nature of Nature"

Do you agree that the Earth is a very dangerous place, and why?

Would we be better off if we settled on the planet Mars?

Chapter 7 'Blue Skies Ahead"

How important is it that we have a specific destination in our travel plans, and in our final destination?

What are some of the ways we can make sure we stay on course all The way Home?

Chapter 8 "The Way"

Some people believe that there are many ways to get to Heaven and to God. What are some of the ways that they believe will get them to heaven?

What does the Word of God promise to those who put their trust in Jesus Christ?

Printed in the United States
By Bookmasters